Mel Bay Presents

Shall We Gather

Hymns Arranged for Hammered Dulcimer

With Harmonies for Hammered Dulcimer and Other Instruments by

Madeline MacNeil

1 2 3 4 5 6 7 8 9 0

Visit us on the Web at http://www.melbay.com — E-mail us at email@melbay.com

Madeline MacNeil is well known for her talents as a singer and performer on the hammered and fretted dulcimers. She is equally well known for the warmth and generosity with which she shares her music and encourages others to play and sing. The silver-haired woman with the golden voice has won the admiration of countless fans across the country. Maddie's twenty-five years as a professional musician have produced many recordings as well as two books for Mel Bay Publications, *You Can Teach Yourself Dulcimer* and *You Can Teach Yourself Hammered Dulcimer.* She arranged the music for Ralph Lee Smith's book for Mel Bay, *Songs of the Wilderness Road.* Maddie publishes *Dulcimer Players News,* which reaches dulcimer enthusiasts throughout the United States and in many other countries.

Her recordings include *All Through the Night, A Place Apart, The Lone Wild Bird, The Crowning of the Year,* and *Heart's Ease,* which won an Indie from the National Association of Independent Record Distributors. For information on *Dulcimer Players News* and Madeline MacNeil's books, videos, and recordings, contact Roots & Branches Music, P.O. Box 2164, Winchester, VA 22604. Phone 540/678-1305, fax 540/678-1151. Web site: www.dpnews.com.

This book is dedicated to the church musicians and choir singers in my family:
my brother James MacNeil, my sister Ruth Anne Troxell, and my brother-in-law Wilson Troxell.
With love and thanks.

My grateful appreciation also goes to Betty Barrett, Doris Ludicke, Stefani Cochran, Ibby Dickson, Karl Sebree, Tabby Finch, Clare Ellis, Robert Barnes, Steve Bullington, Fay Key, and Conrad Hoover.

The watercolor on the cover was painted by Eugene B. Smith, Winchester, Virginia (540/667-6150). The setting is Harper's Ferry, West Virginia behind historic St. Peter's Catholic Church looking toward the Blue Ridge Mountains. The Shenandoah and Potomac Rivers merge at this point.

Cover design by Jeff Lefkowitz, Winchester, Virginia.

Photo of Maddie MacNeil by Bonnie Jacobs, Berryville, Virginia

Contents

Introduction

As a child I spent many an hour playing the piano using the Methodist and Cokesbury hymnals for material. I loved the music, pretending at times that I was directing the choir or playing a huge pipe organ in a cathedral. Later, when I at last stopped squirming and rattling storybooks in church, I began quietly singing harmony to the congregational hymns. Today my love of hymns continues. I purchase the new editions of hymnals and often spend an evening starting at page one.

In creating this collection of hymn arrangements, I couldn't resist fantasizing once more. I could see hammered dulcimer players in church—more than one—playing in harmony. Of course, churches might not have more than one brave hammered dulcimist in the congregation, so these arrangements can be played with other instruments such as flute, guitar, bowed psaltery, and (even though there is no tablature) mountain dulcimer. The harmony parts don't have to be played; the hammered dulcimer melody arrangements are complete in themselves. The stems-up notes provide the melody while the stems-down notes indicate the harmony. Where there are two staves, the stems-up notes on the top staff provide the melody. So people can easily sing the hymns, I kept vocal ranges in mind.

Arpeggios

The squiggly line indicates an arpeggio; three or more notes are played quickly (and sweetly) one at a time, beginning with the bottom note. The three chords in the example would be played DGB, GBD, and GCE.

Note Ranges

Most of the arrangements can be played on a 12/11-course hammered dulcimer (G below middle C is the lowest note on the instrument). Sometimes, particularly when the arrangement is in the key of D, the lower F#, E, and D are used. If you play a 12/11 dulcimer, it is best to ignore the lower notes as most of them are in harmony parts. But a few times you'll find a D# melody note which isn't available on a 12/11. Suggestions are given in those instances for alternative notes to play.

Ledger Lines

To avoid ledger lines in some of the harmony parts, the bass clef is used. I'll remind you of that each time and name those notes as they may be less familiar. But in some of the melodies the lower ledger lines might be confusing, especially when sight-reading. A few times I've named the notes, but suggest that you write in the names of any notes that you seem to miss frequently.

When testing the arrangements, friends and I spent wonderful evenings in my home reading through these beautiful melodies. It wasn't a cathedral; it was even better.

Peace,

Maddie MacNeil

Sweet Hour of Prayer

William Walford, 1845

William B. Bradbury, 1861
arr. by Madeline MacNeil

Sweet hour of prayer, sweet hour of prayer,
The joys I feel, the bliss I share
Of those whose anxious spirits burn
With strong desires for thy return.
With such I hasten to the place
Where God my Savior shows his face,
And gladly take my station there,
And wait for thee, sweet hour of prayer.

Sweet hour of prayer, sweet hour of prayer,
Thy wings shall my petition bear
To him whose truth and faithfulness
Engage the waiting soul to bless.
And since he bids me seek his face,
Believe his word, and trust his grace,
I'll cast on him my every care,
And wait for thee, sweet hour of prayer.

How Great Thou Art

Stuart K. Hine, 1953

Swedish Melody
arr. by Madeline MacNeil

O Lord my God! When I in awe-some won-der con-si-der

Names of some notes, bottom to top

all the works thy hands have made, I see the stars, I hear the might-y

thun-der, thy pow'r through-out the un-i-verse dis-played. Then sings my

soul, my Sav-ior God to thee; how great thou art, how great thou

When through the woods and forest glades I wander,
And hear the birds sing sweetly in the trees;
When I look down from lofty mountain grandeur
And hear the brook, and feel the gentle breeze,
Then sings my soul, my Savior God to thee;
How great thou art, how great thou art.
Then sings my soul, my Savior God to thee;
How great thou art, how great thou art.

And when I think that God, his son not sparing,
Sent him to die, I scarce can take it in;
That on the cross, my burden gladly bearing,
He bled and died to take away my sin;
Chorus

When Christ shall come with shout of acclamation
And take me home, what joy shall fill my heart.
Then I shall bow in humble adoration,
And there proclaim, my God, how great thou art.
Chorus

Come, Thou Fount of Every Blessing

Robert Robinson, ca. 1758

Wyeth's *Repository of Sacred Music,* 1813

arr. by Madeline MacNeil

Come, thou fount of ev-ery bless - ing, tune my heart to sing thy grace; streams of mer - cy, nev - er ceas - ing, call for songs of loud - est praise. Teach me some me - lo - dious son - net, sung by flam - ing tongues a - bove. Praise the

mount! I'm fixed up - on it, mount of thy re - deem - ing love.

Here I raise mine Ebenezer;
Hither by thy help I'm come;
And I hope, by thy good pleasure,
Safely to arrive at home.
Jesus sought me when a stranger,
Wandering from the fold of God;
He, to rescue me from danger,
Interposed his precious blood.

O to grace how great a debtor
Daily I'm constrained to be.
Let thy goodness, like a fetter,
Bind my wandering heart to thee.
Prone to wander, Lord, I feel it,
Prone to leave the God I love;
Here's my heart, O take and seal it,
Seal it for thy courts above.

O Sacred Head, Now Wounded

Words translated by James W. Alexander, 1830

Music adapted by Madeline MacNeil

Hans Leo Hassler, 1601

Harm. Johann Sebastian Bach, 1729

16

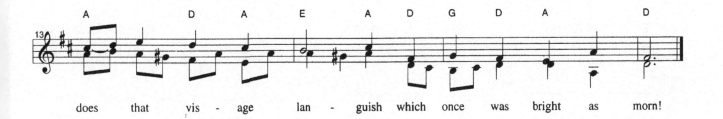

does that vis - age lan - guish which once was bright as morn!

What thou, my Lord, hast suffered Was all for sinners' gain:
Mine, mine was the transgression, But thine the deadly pain.
Lo, here I fall, my Savior! 'Tis I deserve thy place;
Look on me with thy favor, Vouchsafe to me thy grace.

What language shall I borrow To thank thee, dearest friend,
For this thy dying sorrow, Thy pity without end?
O make me think forever, And should I fainting be,
Lord, let me never, never Outlive my love to thee.

Christ the Lord is Risen Today

Charles Wesley, 1739

Lyra Davidica, 1708

arr. by Madeline MacNeil

18

earth re - ply,_____ Al_____ le lu_____ ia!

Harmony part for the last three measures if your dulcimer doesn't have a high E.

Love's redeeming work is done, Alleluia!
Fought the fight, the battle won, Alleluia!
Death in vain forbids him rise, Alleluia!
Christ has opened paradise, Alleluia!

Lives again our glorious king, Alleluia!
Where, O death, is now thy sting? Alleluia!
Once he died our souls to save, Alleluia!
Where's thy victory, boasting grave? Alleluia!

Soar we now where Christ has led, Alleluia!
Following our exalted head, Alleluia!
Made like him, like him we rise, Alleluia!
Ours the cross, the grave, the skies, Alleluia!

Hail the Lord of earth and heaven, Alleluia!
Praise to thee by both be given, Alleluia!
Thee we greet triumphant now, Alleluia!
Hail the resurrection, thou, Alleluia!

King of glory, soul of bliss, Alleluia!
Everlasting life is this, Alleluia!
Thee to know, thy power to prove, Alleluia!
Thus to sing, and thus to love, Alleluia!

For the Beauty of the Earth

Folliott Sandford Pierpoint, 1864

Conrad Kocher, 1838

arr. by Madeline MacNeil

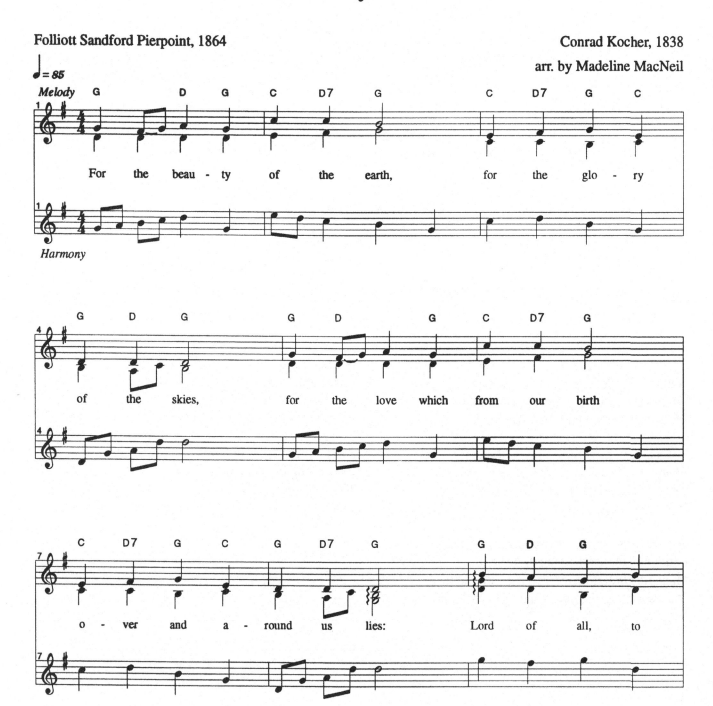

thee   we raise   this   our   hymn   of   grate - ful   praise.

For the beauty of each hour of the day and of the night,
Hill and vale, and tree and flower, sun and moon, and stars of light;
Lord of all, to thee we raise this our hymn of grateful praise.

For the joy of ear and eye, for the heart and mind's delight,
For the mystic harmony linking sense to sound and sight;
Lord of all, to thee we raise this our hymn of grateful praise.

For the joy of human love, brother, sister, parent, child,
Friends on earth and friends above, for all gentle thoughts and mild;
Lord of all, to thee we raise this our hymn of grateful praise.

For thy church, that evermore lifteth holy hands above,
Offering up on every shore her pure sacrifice of love;
Lord of all, to thee we raise this our hymn of grateful praise.

For thyself, best gift divine, to the world so freely given,
For that great, great love of thine, peace on earth, and joy in heaven;
Lord of all, to thee we raise this our hymn of grateful praise.

Be Thou My Vision

Irish words translated by Mary E. Byrne, 1905

Traditional Irish Melody
arr. by Madeline MacNeil

A variation of this melody and harmony begins at measure 17.

Be thou my vi - sion, O Lord of my

heart; nought be all else to me, save that thou

art. Thou my best thought, by

day or by night, wak - ing or

sleep - ing, thy pres - ence my light.

Variation

Be thou my wis - dom, and thou my true word; I ev - er with thee and thou with me, Lord. Heart of my own heart, what - ev - er be - fall, still be my vi - sion, O ru - ler of all.

Ledger Lines Primer

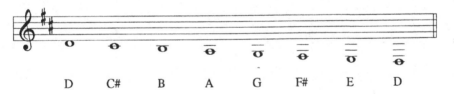

D C# B A G F# E D

12/11 dulcimers don't have the low F#, E, and D. Leave them out when necessary in this arrangement.

Be thou my wisdom, and thou my true word;
I ever with thee and thou with me, Lord;
Thou and thou only, first in my heart,
Great God of heaven, my treasure thou art.

Great God of heaven, my victory won,
May I reach heaven's joys, O bright heaven's sun.
Heart of my own heart, whatever befall,
Still be my vision, O ruler of all.

Praise the Lord, God's Glories Show

Henry Francis Lyte, 1834

Robert Williams, 1817

arr. by Madeline MacNeil

All that see and share God's love. Al - le - lu - ia!

Earth to heaven and heaven to earth, Alleluia!
Tell the wonders, sing God's worth, Alleluia!
Age to age and shore to shore, Alleluia!
Praise God, praise forevermore, Alleluia!

Praise the Lord, great mercies trace, Alleluia!
Praise this providence and grace, Alleluia!
All that God for us has done, Alleluia!
All God sends us through the Son, Alleluia!

Evening Hymns

arr. by Madeline MacNeil

If you don't have a D# to play in measure 3 on the word "draw," change the melody slightly by playing an F#.

Abide With Me

♩ = 85

Modulation to the Key of D

A - bide with me; fast

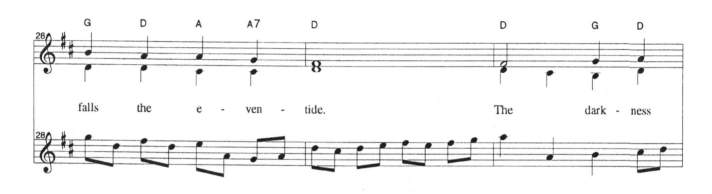

falls the e - ven - tide. The dark - ness

deep - ens; Lord, with me a - bide.

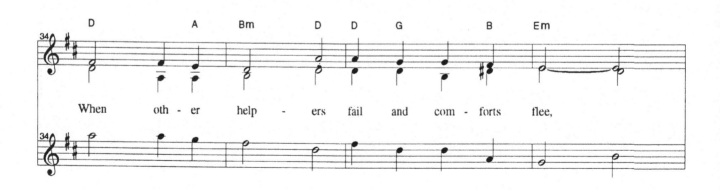

When oth - er help - ers fail and com - forts flee,

28

Help of the help-less, O a-bide with me.

Now the Day is Over

Jesus, give the weary calm and sweet repose;
With thy tenderest blessing may mine eyelids close.

Comfort those who suffer, watching late in pain;
Those who plan some evil from their sin restrain.

When the morning wakens, then may I arise
Pure, and fresh, and sinless in thy holy eyes.

Savior, Again to Thy Dear Name

Grant us thy peace upon our homeward way;
With thee began, with thee shall end the day.
Guard thou the lips from sin, the hearts from shame,
That in this house have called upon thy name.

Grant us thy peace, Lord, through the coming night;
Turn thou for us its darkness into light.
From harm and danger keep thy children free,
For dark and light are both alike to thee.

Grant us thy peace throughout our earthly life,
Our balm in sorrow, and our stay in strife.
Then, when thy voice shall bid our conflict cease,
Call us, O Lord, to thine eternal peace.

Abide With Me

Swift to its close ebbs out life's little day;
Earth's joys grow dim, its glories pass away;
Who, like thyself, my guide and stay can be?
O thou who changest not, abide with me.

I need thy presence every passing hour;
What but thy grace can foil the tempter's power?
Who, like thyself, my guide and stay can be?
Through cloud and sunshine, Lord, abide with me.

I fear no foe, with thee at hand to bless;
Ills have no weight, and tears no bitterness.
Where is death's sting? Where, grave, thy victory?
I triumph still, if thou abide with me.

We Gather Together

Words translated by Theodore Baker, 1894

16th century Dutch melody
arr. by Madeline MacNeil

prais - es to God's name; he for - gets not his own.

Beside us to guide us, our God with us joining,
Ordaining, maintaining his kingdom divine;
So from the beginning the fight we were winning;
Thou, Lord, wast at our side; all glory be thine.

We all do extol thee, thou leader triumphant,
And pray that thou still our defender wilt be.
Let thy congregation escape tribulation;
Thy name be ever praised! O Lord, make us free.

What Wondrous Love is This?

American Folk Hymn ca. 1811

arr. by Madeline MacNeil

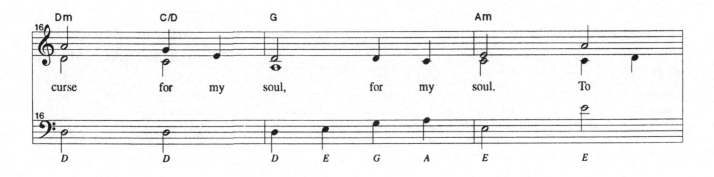

curse   for   my   soul,   for   my   soul.   To

bear   the   dread - ful   curse   for   my   soul!

In the harmony part, roll the hammers (quietly) for four beats in measures 3, 4, 15, and 21 and for two beats in measure 5.

What wondrous love is this, O my soul, O my soul,
What wondrous love is this, O my soul.
What wondrous love is this that caused the Lord of life
To lay aside his crown for my soul, for my soul,
To lay aside his crown for my soul.

To God and to the lamb, I will sing, I will sing.
To God and to the lamb I will sing.
To God and to the lamb who is the great I Am,
while millions join the theme I will sing, I will sing;
While millions join the theme I will sing.

And when from death I'm free I'll sing on, I'll sing on
and when from death I'm free, I'll sing on;
And when from death I'm free, I'll sing and joyful be
And through eternity I'll sing on, I'll sing on,
And through eternity I'll sing on.

He Leadeth Me

Joseph H. Gilmore, 1862

William B. Bradbury, 1864

arr. by Madeline MacNeil

faith - ful fol - lower I would be, for by his hand he lead - eth me.

Sometimes 'mid scenes of deepest gloom, sometimes where Eden's bowers bloom,
By waters still, o'er troubled sea, still 'tis his hand that leadeth me.
He leadeth me, he leadeth me, by his own hand he leadeth me;
His faithful follower I would be, for by his hand he leadeth me.

Lord, I would place my hand in thine, nor ever murmur nor repine;
Content, whatever lot I see, since 'tis my God that leadeth me.
He leadeth me, he leadeth me, by his own hand he leadeth me;
His faithful follower I would be, for by his hand he leadeth me.

And when my task on earth is done, when by thy grace the victory's won,
E'en death's cold wave I will not flee, since God through Jordan leadeth me.
He leadeth me, he leadeth me, by his own hand he leadeth me;
His faithful follower I would be, for by his hand he leadeth me.

In the Garden

Words by C. Austin Miles

C. Austin Miles, 1913

arr. by Madeline MacNeil

He speaks, and the sound of his voice is so sweet the birds hush their singing,
And the melody that he gave to me within my heart is ringing.
And he walks with me, and he talks with me, and he tells me I am his own;
And the joy we share as we tarry there, none other has ever known.

I'd stay in the garden with him though the night around me be falling,
But he bids me go; through the voice of woe his voice to me is calling.
And he walks with me, and he talks with me, and he tells me I am his own;
And the joy we share as we tarry there, none other has ever known.

What a Friend We Have in Jesus

Joseph M. Scriven, 1855

Charles C. Converse, 1868

arr. by Madeline MacNeil

Have we trials and temptations? Is there trouble anywhere?
We should never be discouraged; take it to the Lord in prayer.
Can we find a friend so faithful who will all our sorrows share?
Jesus knows our every weakness; take it to the Lord in prayer.

Are we weak and heavy laden, cumbered with a load of care?
Precious Savior, still our refuge; take it to the Lord in prayer.
Do thy friends despise, forsake thee? Take it to the Lord in prayer.
In his arms he'll take and shield thee; thou wilt find a solace there.

Joyful, Joyful, We Adore Thee

Henry van Dyke, 1907

Ludwig van Beethoven, 1824

arr. by Madeline MacNeil

All thy works with joy surround thee, earth and heaven reflect thy rays,
Stars and angels sing around thee, center of unbroken praise.
Field and forest, vale and mountain, flowery meadow, flashing sea,
Chanting bird and flowing fountain, call us to rejoice in thee.

Thou art giving and forgiving, every blessing, ever blest,
Wellspring of the joy of living, ocean depth of happy rest.
Thou our father, Christ our brother, all who live in love are thine;
Teach us how to love each other, lift us to the joy divine.

Mortals, join the mighty chorus which the morning stars began;
Love divine is reigning o'er us, bringing peace to every land.
Ever singing, march we onward, victors in the midst of strife;
Joyful music leads us sunward, in the triumph song of life.

A Mighty Fortress is Our God

Martin Luther, 1529 (Trans. Frederick Henry Hedge, 1852)

Martin Luther, 1529

arr. by Madeline MacNeil

craft and power are great, and armed with cru - el

hate, on earth is not his e - qual.

Did we in our own strength confide, our striving would be losing,
Were not the right man on our side, the man of God's own choosing.
Dost ask who that may be? Christ Jesus, it is he; Lord Sabaoth, his name,
From age to age the same, and he must win the battle.

And though this world, with devils filled, should threaten to undo us,
We will not fear, for God hath willed his truth to triumph through us.
The Prince of Darkness grim, we tremble not for him;
His rage we can endure, for lo, his doom is sure; one little word shall fell him.

All Beautiful the March of Days

Frances Whitmarsh Wile, 1911

English Melody (Forest Green)

arr. by Madeline MacNeil

laid a si - lent love - li - ness on hill and wood and field.

O'er white expanses sparkling pure the radiant morns unfold;
The solemn splendors of the night burn brighter through the cold;
Life mounts in every throbbing vein, love deepens 'round the hearth.
And clearer sounds the angel hymn, "Good will to all on earth."

O thou from whose unfathomed law the year in beauty flows,
Thyself the vision passing by in crystal and in rose,
Day unto day doth utter speech, and night to night proclaim,
In everchanging words of light, the wonder of thy name.

The words to "O Little Town of Bethlehem," written by Bishop Phillips Brooks in 1866,
fit to this melody. The original folk tune is "The Ploughboy's Dream."

Shall We Gather at the River?

Robert Lowry, 1864

Robert Lowry, 1865
arr. by Madeline MacNeil

The harmony uses the bass clef.

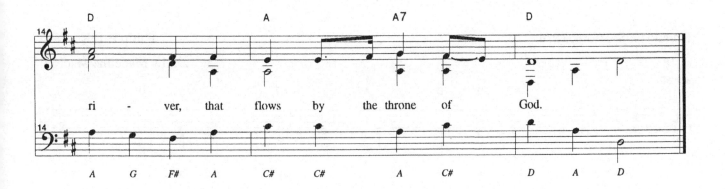

The harmony part, if played on a hammered dulcimer, uses notes below those available
on a 12/11 instrument. You'll need a 15/14 or larger dulcimer.

On the margin of the river, washing up its silver spray,
We will walk and worship ever, all the happy golden day.
Yes, we'll gather at the river, the beautiful, the beautiful river;
Gather with the saints at the river that flows by the throne of God.

Ere we reach the shining river, lay we every burden down;
Grace our spirits will deliver, and provide a robe and crown.
Yes, we'll gather at the river, the beautiful, the beautiful river;
Gather with the saints at the river that flows by the throne of God.

Soon we'll reach the shining river, soon our pilgrimage will cease;
Soon our happy hearts will quiver with the melody of peace.
Yes, we'll gather at the river, the beautiful, the beautiful river;
Gather with the saints at the river that flows by the throne of God.

When Peace, Like a River

Horatio G. Spafford, 1876

Philip P. Bliss, 1876

arr. by Madeline MacNeil

Though Satan should buffet, though trials should come,
Let this blessed assurance control,
That Christ hath regarded my helpless estate,
And hath shed his own blood for my soul.
It is well (It is well) with my soul (with my soul),
It is well, it is well with my soul.

Redeemed! Oh, the bliss of this glorious thought,
My sin, not in part, but the whole,
Is nailed to his cross, and I bear it no more,
Praise the Lord, praise the Lord, O my soul.
It is well (It is well) with my soul (with my soul),
It is well, it is well with my soul.

And, Lord, haste the day when my faith shall be sight,
The clouds be rolled back as a scroll,
The trumpet shall sound, and the Lord shall descend,
Even so, it is well with my soul.
It is well (It is well) with my soul (with my soul),
It is well, it is well with my soul.

Here I Am, Lord

Daniel L. Schutte

Daniel L. Schutte, 1981

arr. by Madeline MacNeil

The first through eighth measures can be used as an introduction or interlude. The melody begins with the ninth measure.

Melody begins here.

I, the Lord of sea and sky,_____ I have heard my peo - ple cry.

All who dwell in dark and sin_____ my hand will

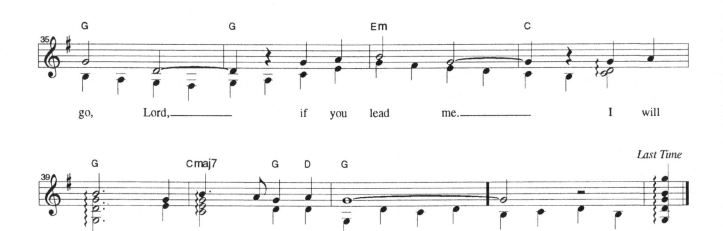

When playing the melody more than once, return to measure 9 after measure 42.
Don't play the last arpeggio (measure 43) each time. Save that for the very end.

I, the Lord of snow and rain, I have borne my people's pain.
I have wept for love of them. They turn away.
I will break their hearts of stone, give them hearts for love alone.
I will speak my word to them. Whom shall I send?
Here I am, Lord. Is it I, Lord? I have heard you calling in the night.
I will go, Lord, if you lead me. I will hold your people in my heart.

I, the Lord of wind and flame, I will tend the poor and lame.
I will set a feast for them. My hand will save.
Finest bread I will provide till their hearts be satisfied.
I will give my life to them. Whom shall I send?
Here I am, Lord. Is it I, Lord? I have heard you calling in the night.
I will go, Lord, if you lead me. I will hold your people in my heart.

Amazing Grace

First published in *Virginia Harmony*, Winchester, Virginia, 1831

John Newton, 1779

Traditional American folk melody

arr. by Madeline MacNeil

blind,   but   now   I   see.

Variation

The harmony part is designed as a background fill—it's there, but not prominent. I had a picture in my mind when arranging; one of the rolling ocean over which Amazing Grace brings its peace.

———————————————

'Twas grace that taught my heart to fear,
And grace my fears relieved;
How precious did that grace appear
The hour I first believed.

Through many dangers, toils, and snares,
I have already come;
'Tis grace has brought me safe thus far,
And grace will lead me home.

When we've been there ten thousand years,
Bright shining as the sun,
We've no less days to sing God's praise
Than when we first begun.

Made in the USA
Monee, IL
09 April 2021